The Christian Way of Life

Eric Alexander was an ordained minister in the Church in Scotland for over 50 years, spending many of those years as senior pastor in the historic St. George's-Tron Church in Glasgow. He studied at the University of Glasgow, graduating Master of Arts in 1954 and Bachelor of Divinity in 1958. Throughout his ministry, and in his retirement years, he preached at conferences such as the Keswick Convention and the Philadelphia Conference on Reformed Theology. He is the author of Our Great God and Savior and Prayer: A Biblical Perspective, both published by Banner of Truth Trust. His sermons can now be heard on the Alliance podcast Hear the Word of God.

©2023 Eric Alexander
Alliance of Confessing Evangelicals
600 Eden Rd., Lancaster, PA 17601.
All rights reserved.
ISBN: 978-0-9852886-7-9

No part of this publication may be reproduced, stored in a retrieval system or transmitted, in any form, or by any means, electronic, mechanical, photocopying, recording or otherwise, without the prior permission of the publisher.

Cover: *Shipping on the Clyde* by Atkinson Grimshaw (1881)

The Christian Way of Life

Spiritual, Personal, Practical *Holiness*

An Exposition of Romans 12–15

Eric Alexander

Contents

CHAPTER 1
Romans 12:1-13   1

CHAPTER 2
Romans 12:14–13:14   21

CHAPTER 3
Romans 14:1-23   41

CHAPTER 4
Romans 15:1-13   59

CHAPTER 1
Romans 12:1-13

Romans 12 to 15 is that section of the Epistle that contains so much of Paul's ethical teaching. In these four chapters, we'll study this passage under the general title of "The Christian Way of Life." In a sense, another title could be what the founders of the Keswick Convention called "scriptural, personal, practical holiness." We greatly need to consider the ethical challenge of biblical holiness (which is always *practical* holiness) and apply it to our whole way of life. Our object, therefore, is to discover the practical implications of that full salvation which God had provided for us in Jesus Christ.

Before beginning our study, we should look to a few introductory matters, starting with the context. If you wanted one word to summarize the theme of this

Epistle, that word would have to be "righteousness." Paul expounds this in four areas:

> **1-3:20** | Righteousness *lacking* in man (3:10 is a key verse in this section);
>
> **3:20-8:39** | Righteousness *provided* by God (5:17 is a key verse, emphasizing the "free gift");
>
> **9:1–11:36** | Righteousness *rejected* by Israel (and here 10:3 is a key verse);
>
> **12:15-15:13** | Righteousness *manifested* in the life of the redeemed (14:17 would be a key verse).

The importance of that context is brought out by that little word we find at the beginning of 12:1 — "therefore." Paul's ethical teaching does not start at chapter 12, where he begins to speak of Christian behavior; it grows out of the whole exposition of the gospel in chapters 1 to 11.

The New Testament knows nothing of a truncated ethical system outside of the gospel. It's been said that you cannot separate Paul's *ethical imperatives* (that is, the demands of the gospel) from his *doctrinal indicatives* (the statements of the gospel).

For without the gospel of redeeming grace, the imperatives become just a counsel of despair. There is the kind of religion that says, "All you need to do is live by the Sermon on the Mount and the Ten Commandments, and do as much of it as you can." From this kind of religion we recoil, and boldly reply, "What I need is not a lecture, but a *Savior*." You see, the unique, distinctive thing about the New Testament ethics is that the New Testament provides a *dynamic* for fulfilling them.

What then is the point of these ethical directives? It's simply this: If the ethic needs a dynamic for its fulfilling, the dynamic needs an ethic for its guidance. You need the work of God's sovereign grace to make you a new man in Christ — that's the steam in the boiler of a locomotive, if you like. But you then need the ethical directives to guide you into the Christian way of life, which (to continue the analogy) is putting the locomotive on the right rails. "Our consciences," says Dr. Packer, "are not educated by gospel but by law." It's part of the bigger question of the relationship between law and gospel in Scripture, never expressed better than by the Puritan Samuel Bolton: "The law drives us to the gospel to learn how to be saved, and the gospel sends us back to the law to learn how to live."

We should also note that Paul is in these chapters still speaking of salvation. For biblical salvation deals with a moral transformation in our character, not just a change in our destiny. Indeed the section to which we turn is really Paul's invitation to enter into all the implications of what God has done for us in Christ. It's not some advanced stage of spirituality attained to by the few; it's the beginning of Christian commitment, it's of the essence of true repentance and faith.

You will notice that verses 1 and 2 begin <u>not</u> with a discussion about the "Christian attitude" to this or that, but with a summons to consecrate our bodies as a living sacrifice to God. The key to the Christian attitude in every issue is this: clarity in the consecration of ourselves wholly to God. You cannot understand the true Christian attitude to anything, outside of this. So we shall have to spend a considerable time on these first two verses, which are quite crucial.

vv. 1–2 | A Summons to Consecration

Paul uses the strong word variously translated "I appeal to you," "I call upon you," "I urge you," "I admonish you," "I call upon you and beseech you." We need to look first at the *ground* of this appeal and then at the *nature* of it.

The Ground of the Appeal

The ground of this appeal is "by the mercies of God." It refers to the whole history of God's dealings with sinful men expounded already in Romans 1 to 11. It refers to the whole scope of what He has done for us in Jesus Christ, and chiefly in His atoning sacrifice and self-offering on the cross. Paul tells us that it's only when we have explored something of the depths of God's mercy shown in Jesus, that this summons to consecration will find an answer in our hearts that is acceptable to God.

Simply put, the reason for trivial, superficial Christian living in ourselves or others is almost always a trivial, superficial view of the sin-bearing death of Jesus. *"Have you not grasped,"* says Paul, *"what redemption means? Do you not know you were bought with a price (cf. 1 Cor. 6:4)?"* As John Calvin said,

> Men will never worship God with a sincere heart, or be roused to fear and obey Him with sufficient zeal, until they properly understand how much they are indebted to His mercy.

The ground of Paul's appeal is the infinite mercies of God, which have found us in such a state of desolation and judgement and have raised us into such a state of blessedness that we have this great testimony: we have been to the fountain that God has opened for sin. We have tasted that the Lord is gracious, we have been justified by His grace, redeemed from sin's bondage, saved from God's wrath, adopted into His family and assured of everlasting life. God has taken us out of the kingdom of darkness when we were enemies of Him, and adopted us — all out of His infinite mercy.

It's important to see that the ground of salvation is not a thing that I have done, but solely the mercy of God, in Jesus Christ. That's not merely a doctrinal issue; it's an issue for practical, Christian living.

The Nature of the Appeal

Regarding the nature or character of this appeal, there are two elements to consider. First, we see that it is an appeal for *the sacrificial offering of a body to God*. The language here is clearly the language of sacrificial ritual.

In the Old Testament, there were two kinds of sacrifice. *Propitiatory* sacrifices atoned for sin (such as were offered on the Day of Atonement). *Dedicatory* offerings, on the other hand, arose out of an experience of God's goodness. We could say that Paul has dealt with the fulfillment of the propitiatory sacrifices in Romans 1–11. He now turns in chapters 12 and following to the implications of dedicatory sacrifices.

What he says about this sacrifice, first of all, is that it's the offering of a body to God. Now, it's often said that the word "body" here symbolizes the totality of man — his personality, character, *etc.* And clearly, Paul does not intend to restrict this consecration just to the physical body. But equally there's a suggestion here, in the way Paul uses the word, that it's *primarily* the physical body that Paul is addressing. This is significant, for the Greek philosophers depreciated the body; their ideal was to get rid of the body altogether. But the biblical view of salvation runs deeply counter to that. God created us in bodies bearing His image, and when He glorifies us at the end of the age, it will be in new bodies that we will serve and worship Him. The Christian hope is in the resurrection of the *body*. Therefore, sanctification must include the body.

Christ is our pattern here. When He consecrated Himself to our salvation, He took His body and offered it to God. True Christian consecration is never a nebulous, mystical, impractical thing, and that's why New Testament teaching about the Christian way of life reaches down to practical details of what you do with your tongue, eyes, hands and so on.

Note also that it is to be a *living* sacrifice. The Old Testament offerings, because they were symbols of divine judgement, were slain. Our sacrifice is to be living, so that our bodies might become the vehicles of the divine will and our lives the object of the divine pleasure. Such offering is our "reasonable service" (Authorized Version), but it seems to me that the Revised Standard and New International versions have caught Paul's intentions better with "spiritual worship." And the New American Standard Bible puts the two together: "your spiritual service of worship." Now that's a good translation, because Paul is probably contrasting the outward ceremonial worship, offering an unwilling slain animal to God, with the inward spiritual worship of a willing, rational living being to Him.

This of course is a great deal of help in understanding the real nature of worship, and Paul at the end of verse 1 does seem to be referring to the common worship of God's people. True worship, says Paul,

> 1. ...derives from a proper view of God's grace in Jesus Christ and is a response to it;
>
> 2. ...is intended to engage our minds;
>
> 3. ...is the presentation of our bodies as a living sacrifice to Him;
>
> 4. ...and is spiritual, engaging the heart.

The second element of this consecration is *the gradual transformation of our character by God*. The appeal of verse 2 is based on the fact already expounded by Paul, that the new age, as it were, has dawned for the Christian. He is to be fashioned, not according to the passing fancies of this world, but according to the patterns of glory which belong to the world to come.

The great temptation, you see, is to be *conformed* instead of *transformed*. It happens in all sorts of subtle ways, often subliminally. You can take up attitudes and standards and criteria, particularly, I would suggest, through the pressure of the media. Have you noticed how easily your spirit becomes inured to the frequent adultery you hear about? The apostle is saying: do not be conformed to this world, but be transformed by the renewing of your mind. Jesus warned, "Do not be like those who seek the things of this world. Seek ye first the kingdom of God, and His righteousness. Be *being* transformed" (that's the literal translation, implying what R.C.H. Lenski called "a constant inner metamorphosis").

The Greek word translated "transformed" is the word used for the transfiguration of our Lord. Interestingly, the only other usage is in 2 Corinthians 3:18: "We all with open face beholding as in a glass the glory of the Lord, are being changed [*i.e.* metamorphosed, transfigured] from one degree of glory to another." Now, this is what Christian character is all about. We are being changed into the image of His glory. The transfiguration of Jesus is in some ways a pattern of that. It is to transfiguration that we are called.

What are the means this moral transformation? Verse 2 tells us: "by the renewing of your mind." The primacy of the mind in biblical sanctification is a great biblical principle. I wonder if you've noticed, that the old order finds sin making its appeal through the senses. The tree was good for food, pleasing to the eyes, and a tree to be desired. The new order in Christ, however, makes its primary appeal through the mind. "Be not mindless, but understanding what the will of the Lord is."

This leads us to the last part of verse 2: "that ye may prove what is the will of God." There are two ideas in this word "prove." One is "discerning in our understanding"; the other, "discovering in our experience." Now, how do we come to know the will of God in these two senses? The *basic* means is the consecration of ourselves to Him. The *specific* means is the renewing of our minds.

First, a disposition to do the will of God is always the basic key to discovering it. We prove the will of God by presenting our bodies a living sacrifice to Him. Second, we do not primarily discern the will of God by hearing voices or "feeling led." Scripture makes primary the relationship between the will of God and the mind of the believer. This is so that we may think our way through to the mind of Christ. How much we need to be reminded of this today!

Some of us have a deep-seated suspicion about the will of God, deeply rooted in our character. We say, "If it's the will of God, I must resign myself to it." Beloved, in Scripture the will of God is something to *run* after, to be pursued like gold, because it is so good and perfect and acceptable for His children!

vv. 3-13 | Good Brothers in the Church

Having laid the foundations in verses 1 and 2, Paul turns in 12:3–13:17 to three spheres of living and testing. In outline, he says that we are able to be good brothers in the church, good neighbors in the world, and good citizens in the State. This remainder of this chapter will address the first of these.

In the church we are to be good brothers. Immediately, at the start of verse 3, Paul establishes the apostolic authority by which he speaks. Do you notice that phrase, "the grace given to me"? Quite clearly, this is not grace in the general sense, but the grace of apostleship, and the appeal of verse 3 has to be seen in the light of the appeal of verse 1. In verse 1 the appeal is on the basis of divine mercy, but in verse 3 it is on the basis of apostolic authority. These appeals are equally binding, and this enshrines a very important principle: Paul's words bear the authority of God. That's what the apostolic truth and authority implies. God has given to the apostles the special responsibility of formulating gospel truth, and the result is in — and constitutes the authority of — the New Testament. You see, we must acknowledge the authority of Paul. It is a vital principle for the authority of Scripture that authority is given to the apostles. The doctrine of authority of Scripture rests partly on this apostolic authority.

Paul, having established this, goes on in verse 3 to point out that so often our thinking about ourselves is wrong. J. B. Phillips translates: "Don't cherish exaggerated ideas of yourself, or of your own importance." One of the evidences of God's grace working in a man's life will be seen in a new attitude to himself. This is where grace changes the whole direction of our thinking and living. "He died for all," says the apostle in 2 Corinthians 5:15, "that those who live should no longer live to themselves but unto Him, who died for them and rose again." I am increasingly persuaded that this brings us to the core of what the Christian life is all about — godly, biblical humility.

But, you notice in verse 3, the biblical alternative to an inflated view of ourselves is not a false depreciation of ourselves, but "to think with sober judgement." Now that's important, because often people think that Uriah Heep, in Charles Dickens' writing, is the closest example of biblical humility — "I'm an 'umble man, Mr. Copperfield," he kept saying. Of course he didn't really believe it. There's often a way to puncture that kind of attitude — you just agree with it! People don't want you to agree with their "Heepishness." And it's not biblical.

To think with "sober judgement" means that the renewal of our minds will produce a realistic assessment of ourselves. We will have the grace to come to terms with how God made us and His providence has shaped us, becoming neither pompous bores nor groveling hypocrites. And the significant thing about verses 3–8 is that the place where this is best achieved is in the true God-given diversity of a living fellowship of God's people. That's why the two key words for finding yourself are "grace" and "faith." The central statement of the passage is in verse 6, "Having gifts that differ according to the grace given to us… ." Now that means that whatever good there is in us is the work of God's grace. How can I be inflated by this? It is the grace of God which has produced my gifts, and therefore I am able to recognize that. I can avoid the blasphemous affront of using God's gifts as a means of self-display. The true seedbed of biblical humility is the doctrine of grace.

Now, you will notice that in the gifted body of Christ there is equality of dignity and diversity of function, compared in verses 4 and 5 to the human body. Our own God-given function is discovered by a recognition of God's grace, and an exercise of God-given faith. Notice the end of verse 3 "according to the measure of faith …," and verse 6, "in proportion to our faith." (Probably not so much saving faith, as *serving* faith.) This means that I must beware not only of pride, but of unbelief. That's important for our own well-being, for it helps us to become truly ourselves. And it's important for the well-being of the church, for the church will never become what God meant it to be, if, through unbelief, I am settling for being less than what God meant me to be. It's the glory, you see, of that picture of the body. And you have a place in that body. You dare not, by unbelief, miss God's place in it for you. In this way, Paul urges every member of the body (verses 6-8) to exercise precisely the gift that God has given them.

The list of gifts is not really a list of offices, but a series of examples to show how varied the gifts are and how they are to be exercised. Do you notice that there are seven in all? Two are directed to the gift itself, and two to the person. "...If prophecy," (verse 6), "let him prophesy in proportion to faith; if service, in serving." These are the gifts themselves. Then follow the persons – he who exhorts, contributes, gives aid, etc. The gifts are to be exercised again in proportion to faith. The correct translation is probably, "According to the proportion or analogy of *the* faith." And I think that Paul is quite simply saying here that whatever is uttered as coming from God must be consistent with the rest of revealed truth. To the prophet he says: don't go outside God's truth. Then, service; probably a reference to the deacons. Then teaching, the expounding of revealed truth. Let the teacher stick to his last, says Paul; be not a speculator but an expositor. The exhorter, suggests the New International Version, is possibly the encourager. He who contributes — this is a reference to personal giving, not to the official church collection. Let it be without mixed motives, Paul is probably counseling. The sixth gift is "giving aid" (RSV), but it's probably leadership. How much we need that gift to be exercised in the church today.

The last gift is the showing of mercy, which is really that quality of godly care which ought to mark a real fellowship. If that is your gift, says Paul, exercise it with cheerfulness. And how helpful it is, when people have found their way into God's perfect destiny for them in this sense.

Verse 9 marks a new section of the chapter. It is a turning of our attention man-wards, into the area of relationships, where our sanctification is so often tested. Verse 9 lays down the universal obligation, having spelt out the diverse gifts. "Let love be genuine." That love is of course a divine and not a human thing; a supernatural, rather than a natural grace, the first fruit of the Holy Spirit. It's the hallmark of discipleship, according to Jesus: "By this shall all men know that you are My disciples, if you love one another." The whole thought of verses 9 to 13 is really of a life which goes out to others in selfless devotion and service.

Concerning this love, notice first that it must be real, without hypocrisy (verse 9). It must be moral. It must be zealous for the good of others. Secondly, it is a driving zeal to love and care (vv. 10, 11). Paul brings this to a great climax at the end of verse 13, where he speaks of hospitality. What is this love in relation to others that is to be seen in our lives in consecrated Christian living? It is hospitality. That word belongs to the same family as "hospital," the place for the care of sick and wounded. What Paul is pleading for is a life that is a hospital for the sick and wounded and needy in the world. That's what consecrated Christian living really means in relation to others. God make our lives like hospitals!

CHAPTER 2
Romans 12:14–13:14

Now the apostle broadens his focus to include the wider world around us; the unbelieving and frequently hostile world.

vv. 14–21 | Good Neighbors in the World

Verse 9, as we have seen, introduces love as the universal obligation that we owe both to our fellow Christians in a "family" sense, and to the world even when it persecutes us. This is what is to control all our relationships. You will notice tremendous similarities and parallels with the Sermon on the Mount. "Love your enemies," says Jesus (Matthew 5:44): "Bless those who persecute you," says Paul (verse 14).

In Scripture, "bless" can mean different things. When we bless God, we give Him the praise and glory which He deserves. When God blesses us, He bestows on us the grace which we do not deserve. When we bless other people, we desire for them the riches of God's grace irrespective of what they deserve. That's what it means to bless those who persecute you.

The second half of the verse reinforces this with an appeal that the blessing should be whole-hearted and not half-mixed with cursing. You remember James' warning, about the mouth out of which proceeds both blessing and cursing (3:8–12)? What Paul is saying is that the attitude we are to have to our enemies who persecute us is unmixed desire for their blessing, ruling out bitterness and animosities and harbored resentments. This of course is precisely what Jesus teaches in the Sermon on the Mount, and the reason he gives is, "that you may be children of your Father." In other words, this is what God is like. Says Calvin:

> "I grant that this is hard and quite contrary to human nature; but there is nothing so arduous that

it cannot be overcome by the power of God. And this we shall never lack, provided we do not neglect to pray for it."

The results of this basic attitude described in verse 14 are to be seen in our obedience to the demands of verses 15 to 21. For example, verse 15; if I desire God's blessing on somebody, then I will genuinely rejoice when they receive it, and genuinely mourn when they are denied it. That is something the world never does. It is supernatural to rejoice, with no tinge of jealousy, when others are being blessed, particularly if we do not like them. And it is a very important test as to whether we are concerned for the glory of God or for our own little ego or little show. We need to pray that God will give us that detachment from other things, for His glory.

This reinforces to us how utterly vital it is to transform our attitudes, because so much of the teaching up to the end of chapter 12 depends on a spirit of self-forgetfulness. And that spirit opposes three things of which verse 16 speaks. The first is *disharmony*. "Live in harmony with one another," says verse 16. R. C. H. Lenski points out that this is a harmony deriving from something deeper than unanimity of mind. I am to want for you what, if I were in your position, I would want for myself. Self-interest, you see, destroys harmony. Think what our fellowship would be like if we were really desiring for others what we would most like for ourselves, were we in their position!

Second, self-forgetfulness opposes all forms of *snobbery*. "Do not be haughty, but associate with the lowly." The tendency in a godless world is to aspire to the society of those you conceive to be above you, and to despise those you conceive to be below you. This is self-interest, and it's perilously easy to harbor that spirit secretly, even if we would never openly admit to it. I have no hesitation in saying that all forms of snobbery are obnoxious to the God who was born in a shed, raised as a manual worker, and for much of His life was homeless and of no fixed abode. You can't sanctify snobbery. You can only mortify it.

The third thing that self-forgetfulness rules out is *vanity*. I'm inclined to think that what is meant is intellectual vanity — snobbery applied to wisdom. Closely allied to it is *conceit*, which makes it impossible for us to learn from others.

You can see how each of these derives from self-interest. Moving out into every sphere of life, self-interest affects us in these various ways, and these are the three areas the apostle puts his finger on.

Verses 17 to 21 take this attitude of self-forgetfulness and apply it to the case of the Christian who has suffered injury or abuse of some sort or other, and explain how he is to react to it. These verses have often been misunderstood, misapplied, and misused as a biblical basis for rejecting retributory punishment (i.e. punishment as the just reward for wrongdoing). People often quote, "Repay no one evil for evil." In a similar manner, these verses are also used to reject capital punishment.

Now, whatever you think about capital punishment, you cannot deduce a view of it from these verses. I want to suggest to you that these verses are not concerned really with such issues at all. The misunderstanding arises from a failure to grasp that these verses speak of *personal* relationships, not the public administration of justice to which we come in chapter 13. It's a distinction that needs to be carefully kept in mind.

There are two great principles in these verses which Paul sets down for us, beginning in verse 17. Firstly, the Christian must never behave as though he were a law court exacting justice. "Repay no one evil for evil" means not getting your own back. In its place, in the second half of verse 17, we find a spirit concerned for a standard of conduct which will commend Christ to our unbelieving neighbors: "take thought for what is noble in the sight of all." And of course, the example is Jesus, who, when He suffered, threatened not. The corollary to the principle of not behaving as if one were a law court is that the law court itself must never behave as if it were an individual, dealing with personal relationships and not matters of public justice.

The second great principle that Paul raises is, the Christian must never behave as though he were God, taking vengeance (verse 19). Vengeance is a function that God has reserved exclusively for Himself. There are occasions when we find our patience tried. Is that not so? We cannot understand how people "get off with this kind of thing." Of course, this is the age-old problem of the ungodly, with which the Psalmist wrestles in Psalm 73. The biblical command, you see, is to leave it to God.

Now, failure to do that is really the kind of unbelief which shows that we are not sure enough of God to be able to trust Him for this — that we are more sure of ourselves, and our ability to take matters into our own hands. Professor John Murray sees this issue as touching the essence of piety, which, he says, is "turning everything over to God." Whereas the essence of impiety is to try to take the place of God and take things into our own hands.

Instead of acting the law court or acting God, therefore, we are to act the peacemaker (verse 18). It may not always be possible, but Paul says "if it be possible." "The most peaceful Christian," wrote Martin Luther, "may be set upon by snarling, biting dogs." Paul's point is that, if peace is broken, you should never be the cause of it for your own sake. "Blessed are the peacemakers," says Jesus, in terms of personal relationships. We need to ask ourselves:

Am I the kind of person in a fellowship who is a peacemaker, or a peace-breaker? The cause of disquiet and unrest is so often our wounded pride or our thoughtless selfishness.

Finally, says Paul, we are to act the conqueror (verses 20 and 21). Paul moves from the negative attitude (the refraining from acting against our enemy or maintaining the peace) to the positive act of seeking to change him. How? That's the great question. If we show the same attitude to the worldling as he shows to us, he has conquered us. That's all that has happened. You may have said to yourself, "Oh, if I'd just thought of that cutting barb, I could really have pierced him with — but I thought of it too late!" You lament your "slow-thinking" because you wanted to satisfy your selfish pride. But if you had remembered, he would have conquered you, not you him. So Paul says, "If your enemy is hungry, feed him; if he is thirsty, give him to drink, for by doing so you will heap coals of fire on his head. Do not be overcome by evil, but overcome evil with good." That's the significance of the phrase "heap burning coals upon his head" (a quotation from Proverbs 25:21–22).

13:1–7 | Good Citizens in the State

The apostle now takes a new direction in considering the Christian way of life. Chapter 13 can be seen as containing three obligations linked to three themes:

> **1-7** | the theme of authority and our relationship to the State;
>
> **8-10** | the theme of love and our obligation to the law to fulfill it;
>
> **11-14** | the theme of the return of our Lord and our obligation to holiness in the light of it.

We turn now to the theme of authority and the obligation of civil obedience (13:1-7). "Authority" occurs five times in the Revised Standard Version of these verses. The subject is very topical for us since one of the facts of modern life is a revolt against authority of all kinds, and its breakdown in certain areas. Paul talks a great deal about authority. "Let every person be subject to the governing authorities.

For there is no authority except from God...." The basic fact he wants to underline is that authority, as an idea, was invented by God. That's what he is saying in verse 1.

That doesn't mean that God is pleased with everybody who exercises authority. It *does* mean that God is the author of the idea. The Christian does not blindly praise authority however it is exercised, but he does recognize its origin. His attitude to authority will be one of respect and submission, not just because it is a good thing for society, but because it is our duty before God.

Let me explain what I mean. To deny authority is really to deny two fundamental things about man: his *creatureliness* and his *fallenness*.

God's authority over us evidences our creatureliness. He made us to live in such a way that we need His authority in our lives. It was true in man's un-fallen state, and man was put into Eden with authoritative instructions on how to live aright. God's delegation of His authority in the civil, domestic and commercial spheres which you find in the giving of the Law and in so many other places in

Scripture, is a hedge against our sinfulness, and the tendency within us to rebel against authority. It's these things which are being denied in the current revolt against established authority. This is one of the reasons why it is so important to have a truly biblical view of man. In the intellectual world, the libertarian repudiates all intellectual authority over man, except that which self-authenticates. In the social realm, even the permissive society is rejected by some people as a shade too paternalistic! Instead there is the alternative society, in which there is no authority and everybody is free to make up his own mind. They think it's a modern idea! Of course, the Book of Judges ends with the statement that "every man did that which was right in his own eyes." In such a society, for example, all censorship is abolished, even for the very young. And the implication is that man is not a creature or that he is not a sinner.

Let me share five propositions to sum up what I think the apostle is saying in these verses. First, the ultimate authority, and the only universal and absolute one, is God (verse 1). Ultimately all men will be answerable to God, which has already been implied in the last section of chapter 12. It's been laid down in Genesis 1 to 3 (man is a creature), and reinforced at Sinai in the giving of the Law. And it's visibly demonstrated, supremely, "when every knee shall bow and every tongue confess that Jesus Christ is Lord."

Second, God delegates some of His authority. He passes it on to certain people saying "Use that, for Me." Do you notice at the end of verse 1, that the authorities that exist "have been instituted by God"? And also in verses 4 and 6. The principle extends to all proper spheres, including (it seems to me, from Scripture) to husbands in marriage, parents within the family, and masters within the servant/master relationship — however you interpret that for modern times. Let me say again, it does not imply that God is pleased with those who abuse authority given them.

Third, to resist authority is to resist God (verse 2). This is how Scripture teaches us to view rebellion against instituted authority: It is like rebellion against God.

Fourth, such rebellion merits punishment (verses 2 and 4). It seems to me inescapable to conclude this is so. Laws always have to be accompanied by penalties for breaking them. Clearly, this biblical doctrine of punishment is neither primarily reformative ("Don't do it again"), nor is it primarily a deterrent ("Let that be a lesson to others"); it is retributive ("This is the just reward for your crime").

The question obviously arises at this point: Is all resistance to authority therefore forbidden? This is a pressing question in our modern world, especially in the international sphere.

To this question we must answer, "No." There is indeed an important exception: Governing authority may be resisted when it commands us to disobey God. In verse 7 Paul urges, "Pay all of them their dues" (a reflection of Jesus' words, "Render to Caesar"). But if Caesar demands the things that are God's, then the answer must be that of Peter in Acts 5: "We ought to obey God, rather than men." As Sir Thomas Taylor wrote,

> "In certain circumstances, disobedience to the State may not only be a right, but a duty. This has been

classical Christian doctrine ever since the apostle declared that they ought to obey God rather than men."

We need to think some of these things through, however briefly. Does this mean that a Christian can support and engage in violent revolution? It's a real issue in many parts of the world today.

I would suggest, on both biblical and theological grounds, that the answer is "No." On biblical grounds, I would want to point out that the only two instances of civil disobedience, in Acts 5 and Revelation 13, are concerned with a defense of the liberty to worship God. Paul, in 1 Timothy 2:2, urges us to pray for all in authority, with this in view.

Moreover, I would point out that Jesus turned down the clamor of the masses to become a violent revolutionary (John 6:15). He said that His kingship was not brought about by this means. On theological grounds, I would want to point out further that sin is endemic in man's nature, not in his environment. The root of injustice is in the heart of men, and that's why so many revolutions end in disappointment and violence ends in despair.

Returning now to our propositions, we must fifthly and finally recognize that the institution of authority was meant by God for our greater good and the common well-being (verses 3 and 4). Now, you can't just restrict that to Christian governments, or even those with Christian orientations, because in the Old Testament you find God speaking through Jeremiah to the people of Israel: "Serve the King of Babylon, and live." That meant going into captivity., and yet God sent them there. We need to recognize that authority and freedom are not alternatives; authority makes true freedom possible.

Young people in particular need to hear this: The alternative to authority is not liberty, but anarchy, which is then followed by tyranny. This is what makes the present age's suspicion of and revolt against authority so alarming. The only place where true freedom is to be found is in bondage to Jesus Christ and total submission to the authority of His Lordship. And that involves submission to the authority of His word, which bids us to be submitted to the governing authority. This is the Christian way of life.

13:8-10 | The Obligation of Love to Neighbor

Permit me to now draw your attention to how Paul underlines this whole concept of obligation in relation to love. Notice he moves from verse 7, the paying of what is due, to verse 8, the obligation of love. Notice how many times the word "due" appears in verse 7. He is speaking there about the whole realm of duty. You have a duty, he says, to discharge these obligations. But even more binding is the duty of love.

The idea of love being an obligation or duty is one that many people find hard to accept. How can I be under obligation to love anybody? Two misunderstandings prompt this, I think. The first is a misunderstanding of the nature of Christian love. We tend to think of it as a kind of feeling, a sort of afflatus come upon us, which we are incapable of calling up or dismissing. But Christian love in the New Testament is regarding and dealing with people as God has regarded and dealt with us; it has a moral content. It is not (in John Stott's excellent contrast) the victim of our emotions, but the servant of our will.

The Christian Way of Life

The other misunderstanding is of the whole place of *duty* in the Christian life. May I say that I think we as evangelicals are weak in this whole area of duty and obligation. We quote "Render unto Caesar the things that are Caesar's" — and we stop there. But Jesus didn't! "And render unto God the things that are God's." In other words, just as you have a duty to pay your taxes, you have an obligation to God to love your neighbor. Now you don't pay your taxes according to your emotional feelings, but we so often imagine that that's the way we are called to live the Christian life. But, for example, prayer is a duty. "Men ought always to pray, and not to faint." We are called on by God to pray. As Samuel said to the people, "God forbid that I should sin against the Lord in ceasing to pray for you" (1 Samuel 12:23).

We need to learn this place of duty. Notice, Paul does not say (verses 8-10) that law is love, or that love replaces law. He says, "Love fulfills the law." Remember Jesus' words: "If you love me, keep my commandments." Love will prevent us breaking the law, says Paul, mentioning four specific areas at the end of verse 9. There we find this is the kind of love which puts our neighbor in place of ourself.

13:11-14 | Obligations in Light of the Great Day

They are obligations to holiness of life. Paul is, as it were, like the town crier, calling on men to recognize what the hour is. The great day is coming.

These two chapters, 12 and 13, taken together begin and end with an exhortation, an appeal. The first, as we have seen, is in 12:1-2, based on the display of God's mercy in Jesus Christ. Something that lay in the past, for these Christians at Rome. And the appeal there is to consecrate our bodies as a living sacrifice to Him.

Now this closing appeal at the end of chapter 13 is based on something that lies ahead of them, the display of God's full glory in salvation when the day dawns for Christ's appearing. The appeal is to holy living, the casting off of the works of darkness, the putting on of the armor of light. It's significant that here, as elsewhere in Scripture, both of the appearings of the Lord Jesus Christ are used as incentives to holiness. "Our salvation is nearer than when we believed." You notice, the apostle speaks of salvation in the broader sense that we mentioned in our previous study. It's not something finished with, in the here and now. We have of course received full salvation in Jesus Christ, but, there is something infinitely more that God has yet to do for us. That's the glorious thing about being a child of God! The best is yet to be. The dawn is yet to break. The glory is yet to come.

That day is the day to which we, and the whole creation, and the whole universe, are moving. The climax of the ages will come on that day. We belong to that age, says Paul. That's where you have your roots; that's where your true inheritance is. Your real life lies in the coming King. You'll see what salvation is all about, and the world will see it, when He appears in His infinite glory. And He will be admired by all them that believe.

But, you see, that's the point. That day is hastening on. And the great danger, my beloved, is that we grow careless. It's so easy for us to slumber, to get careless about the glory of God, the health of our soul, the quality of our Christian testimony, and the state of a man without Christ. *Slumbering*. And the apostle says, "The night is far spent, the day is at hand: let us therefore cast off the works of darkness, and let us put on the armor of light."

You see the contrast: works of *darkness*, armor of *light*. These conflicting labels are very significant. The works of darkness are expounded in verse 13. The armor speaks of the fact that in these last days, as the dawn is about to break, the battle will grow no less fierce — so put on the armor.

What is this armor? It is expounded in verse 14. It isn't just the opposite moral quality to the degrading works of darkness. To put on the armor of light is to put on *the Lord Jesus Christ*. It is nothing less than the moral glory and the moral beauty of our Lord Jesus that we are to be wearing as we move towards the day of His return.

CHAPTER 3
Romans 14:1-23

The theme of chapter 14 is *the Christian way of life in relation to our attitudes to others over doubtful things*. It is in a sense a new theme, though the apostle is still working out the implications for Christian behavior of a consecrated body, a renewed mind, and a transformed character. And the theme of chapter 14 flows on from the obligation of Christian love which concerns Paul in 13:8. Much of chapters 12 and 13 dealt with various relationships which truly test our consecration to God, Yet in chapter 14, Paul turns to a relationship which exists within the fellowship of the church between true believers—not now in the alien world, but *in the church*. This is our relationship with other Christians, with whom we differ over non-essentials, a topic of great relevance to the Christian church today.

What Paul is talking about in verses 1-3 is not just a remote situation, but one that exists in almost every Christian fellowship in every generation. Among fellow Christians there will always be differences of opinion. The danger is that these areas of difference will become like areas of dry tinder into which the devil just loves to throw a match. And we are not unfamiliar with the blazing fires that result.

We therefore need to learn from God how to relate to those with whom we differ. And I would like us to have our thinking directed into three vital questions which we need to ask of this somewhat difficult chapter.

1. What Are "Doubtful Issues"?

Perhaps I can begin by clarifying what they are *not*. Paul is not referring to those who differ over the truth of the gospel, which is never referred to as "doubtful" in the New Testament. Tolerance and welcome, which Paul urges us to give to those with different opinions, are the very reverse of what he extends to those who differ over the centralities of the gospel. As he said to the Galatians (1:9), "If any man preach any other gospel than that which we have preached unto you, let him be anathema." Paul is wholly intolerant and unwelcoming to any distortion of the gospel.

Neither is Paul speaking of a difference of opinion over matters of Christian behavior where clear-cut commands from God exist; that is, in matters of ordinary morality, or Christian duty. For such issues there is no room for debate. Some things are not negotiable; because one thing is right, and another is wrong. That's important to grasp in an age which is intolerant of dogmatism, and television programs (especially religious ones, I may add) give assent to two diametrically opposed views.

No, Paul is not advocating a mushy tolerance about everything with convictions about nothing. He is dealing not with centralities, but with *marginal* issues. Paul in no way opposes true spiritual discernment, but rather that carping critical spirit which loves an argument (especially over trivia). This has tended to be an evangelical phenomenon.

What then are these marginal issues? They seem to be of two kinds: *Matters of personal behavior,* particularly related to *special diets* (verse 2); and *matters of church observance*, particularly related to *special days* (verse 5). These are areas where Scripture is either silent or not dogmatic, areas of speculation rather than revelation.

Special Diets

One context of this is probably Jewish dietary laws. Not Old Testament dietary laws — that's a different thing. They didn't forbid meat eating in general. But the church historian Josephus tells us that some Jews in Rome followed a strict vegetarian diet. It was a Jewish tradition rather than an Old Testament law. Another possibility is that some of these people were influenced by the Essene sect, of which you will have heard because the Dead Sea Scrolls came from them. Some of the Essenes had longstanding traditional laws about meat eating.

A second context would perhaps be the offering of meat to idols. Much butcher's meat in those days would have been so offered, and it was almost impossible to tell if what you were eating had been offered to idols. Now some people would have said, "So what? Christ has freed us from bondage, and these idols are dead figures anyway." Others, on the other hand, would have said, "How can we possibly eat this meat? We will rather be vegetarians."

Special Days

This issue seems to have been the ceremonial holy days of the levitical institution. Some felt that they should continue to keep the solemn days and festivals and other special days; I think it's important to say here that Paul can hardly be referring to the Christian Lord's day, for the Sabbath principle belongs to the moral law in the decalogue, not the ceremonial law. Not only so, but it is a creation ordinance preceding the moral law. In the New Testament it is perpetual recurring memorial to Jesus' resurrection: the early church gathered to break bread on that day (Acts 20:7). So I suggest that Paul is instead referring to the high days and holy days, because otherwise, he would be calling somebody who was concerned to keep the moral law, the weaker brother.

I must add that I think Paul *is* referring here to Sabbatarianism in some of its odder forms. The modern equivalent might for instance be special days like Good Friday. You will nowhere in Scripture find Good Friday to be a special day for Christians to observe; yet, I have friend who is a minister who will *never* marry somebody on Good Friday, as he regards it as a very special day. This may be a particular issue. And I suppose, if you want an example that brings the two questions of diets and days together, it might be the man who will not eat meat on Friday.

But Paul's principle applies to all kinds of marginal issues, where, I say again, Scripture is silent and tradition is vocal, whether it be national, ecclesiastical, cultural or family traditions. They all affect us deeply, some of them become dogma inadvertently, and that's one of the grave dangers of the situation.

There are cultural backgrounds as well. In Indonesia, in Java, I went into a pastors' conference session, and could hardly see any of the men — godly men mightily used in Indonesia — because they were all smoking. Well, you see, it was from the Dutch cultural tradition which was part of their lives. I didn't think it was helpful to them, but it was a cultural factor. There are many less important things than these that have become part of the fiber of our lives. One of the important themes of chapter 14 is getting the really important things put first.

2. To Whom Does the Apostle Refer?

We can answer this more briefly. They're described in 14:1 as "the weak." And in 15:1, "We who are strong ought to bear with the failings of the weak." The weak may be over-scrupulous Christians from a Jewish background on one hand; and on the other, Gentile converts. What we know for sure is that the weak brother (and here may be a surprise for you) is the one who has most scruples and is most tender in his conscience about all these do's and don'ts. We tend to think, don't we, that the man who won't do this or that, and has scruples about almost every detail of these cultural matters, is the strong Christian. But Paul says he is the *weak* one (verse 2). The temptation is to get caught up in the details of such issues as these, become distracted from the things that are central, and be disabled for serving God in the things which really do matter.

3. What Counsel Does the Apostle Give?

This is our main theme in this study. What is the Christian way of life in these circumstances? Well, Paul lays down seven basic and important principles of very wide application over doubtful issues.

The first is this: *Welcome those whom God welcomes* (verses 1 and 3, and 15:7). You will notice the irony in the last part of verse 3. Here are some believers holding such a brother at arm's length, being cold towards him, refusing him fellowship and membership within the church or, more likely, just refusing to open their hearts to him totally without reservation to show him true, warm, generous Christian love and welcome. Because he doesn't dot all their ecclesiastical i's and stroke their t's exactly as they do! Yet God has welcomed him; Christ has welcomed him; and the problem is therefore that you're out of sorts with God and His Son, because you're holding back.

Now here's the principle, and I quote to you the words of that great commentator on Romans, Charles Hodge: "If God has not made it a barrier to communion with Him, we dare not make it a barrier to fellowship with us." It's not just a question of being "holier-than-thou." It's a question of being "holier-than-God."

The welcome has two qualifications. Verse 1, "but not for disputes over opinions." Don't welcome him in just to eat him up. Do not make the church of God a place for arguments about stupidities and trivialities. And the second qualification is: this is not to be a cold, grudging welcome, but one which exemplifies the warmth and depth, and genuineness of the love of God in Jesus Christ.

The second principle is: *Avoid either judging or despising others* (verses 3 and 4). There are two tendencies, further amplified in verses 10 to 13. The weak brother tends to sit in judgement on the strong, who doesn't have such scruples as himself. It is easy, as James Denny pointed out, to lapse from scrupulousness about one's own conduct to pharisaism about that of others. The strong brother, on the other hand, tends to despise the weak brother, who in his eyes is just a pathetic crank.

Behind both attitudes is the ugly spirit of which Jesus warned in Matthew 7 (as I've said, Romans 12 to 14 and the Sermon on the Mount have a great deal in common); the spirit of censorious criticism, which Paul condemns in verse 10.

Paul states three things that are wrong about this spirit which so often arises from these marginal matters, about which Scripture is not dogmatic. In verse 3 he says it is *judgement on the wrong issues*. It is judgement of trivia, and it's significant that in Matthew 7 this is what Jesus puts his finger on. "Why do you say to your brother, 'Let me take the speck out of your eye'?" A speck is something you have to look for consciously. It's minutiae, trivia. It's judgement by *shibboleth* (the word we find in the story of Judges 12 — look it up!). Paul is saying that here we have judgement on the basis of shibboleth. So much of our judging and despising of others is on the basis of whether we can pronounce our shibboleth. That's one of the applications of verse 17.

But the other major error of this judgement is that it is *judgement by the wrong people*. Look at verses 4 and 10. Verse 4 implies that judging your brother is like interfering in the domestic affairs of someone else's family. The standard that will be applied to your brother is the standard his own master sets and his own master is Christ. And He will not judge on the basis of trivia. If we judge we condemn one whom the Lord has made to stand (verse 4). So the real controversy is not between you and your brother, but between you and his Lord.

Verses 10 to 12 take this a stage further: Paul says that it is *judgement at the wrong time*. We are anticipating the judgement seat of God. At that judgement seat we shall all have to give an account of ourselves. That means our censorious word and our despising spirit will be judged before God. It is not for my brother's scruples or absence of them that I will have to answer, but my own.

Here is the third principle: *Think things through for yourself* (verse 5). It's simply an extension of Paul's appeal in 12:1-2, for conduct which springs from a renewed mind. Christian conduct is not a case of an endless list of do's and don'ts. It is not to be moulded by taboos and prejudices. It is to be decided by gaining the mind of Christ on every issue, thinking through them with a consecrated, biblical mind.

Now this is of great importance. There is a mindlessness about many supposedly Christian attitudes which can lead you away from Christian liberty in two directions. On one hand it can lead you to license because "everybody's doing it." I'm amazed at the number of Christians who say, "Of course, all Christians are doing this-or-that nowadays." The clear answer should be, "So what?"

On the other hand, this mindlessness can lead you into legalism, because—at least in your circle—*nobody's* doing it. Paul says, "Be fully convinced in your own mind." He is not interested in a mere set of rules for outward conformity; he is interested in the renewal of Christian character through renewing of the mind. This is what God has given us His word for, to enable us to think things through with the mind of Christ. It furnishes us with "just principles to direct our conduct," as John Newton said. This is one of the vital reasons for being under a consistent ministry of the word of God. Through this, God shapes our minds and forms our thinking, so that we think things through with the mind of God.

This is not to say that there are no standards, or that one man's opinion is as good as another's. That's not Paul's point. The standards are the standards by which our judgement is to be formed: the authority of Scripture and the lordship of Christ.

This leads to the fourth principle: live under *the lordship of Christ* (vv. 6 to 9). Again and again, it is honoring the Lord, and living to the Lord, of which Paul speaks, until the great climax in verse 9. Our liberty is to be controlled by Christ's lordship. You will notice, *we* do not make Jesus Lord. God the Father has already done this, it is the reward for Jesus' humiliation. This lordship he has achieved by His death and His resurrection.

If I were to leave the last word of verse 9 blank, and say to you, "To this end Christ died and lived again, that He might be…," I'm sure you would say, "Savior." But Paul says, "Lord." It has been said that it's possible to have Jesus as your Savior but not as your Lord. "I didn't accept Him as Lord when I accepted Him first as Savior." But I want to say to you, the New Testament knows nothing of that strange phenomenon! There is only one Jesus Christ, who is both Lord and Savior.

We *acknowledge* His lordship. It is a fact before we discover it. He has the right to rule over our lives. From verse 6 onwards, this touches almost every area Paul is dealing with. The direction of the whole of life is to be toward the lordship of Jesus.

This is the freedom that the gospel brings: freedom to obey Him whose service is perfect. As Gifford has written, "If it should seem irksome to bow so completely to the lordship of Christ, let us remind ourselves it is not a philosophy or an abstraction, far less a tyrant, to whom we give homage, but the greatest lover in the whole universe." The fact of my liberty is controlled and defined by the fact of Christ's lordship.

Now, to the fifth principle: *Let liberty be controlled by love.* From verse 13, the apostle urges us that the Christian way of life in relation to those with whom we differ over unimportant issues is to be marked not by condemnation of them but by consideration of them. There is a play of meanings in verse 13 for the word "judge." Paul juxtaposes a prohibition of judgement by condemnation, with a command to apply our judgement of reason to avoid giving offense. The word for "hindrance" really means the springing of a trap — a death trap, suggests Lenski. Therefore, we are to resolve never to be the cause of hurt or harm to our brother, but to be sensitive by God's grace to what will help him and what will hinder him.

As Christians, we live under the law of liberty *and* the law of love. We need to be able to hold these two together in all our relationships with other people, particularly in this area. Freedom is what Christ has liberated us for, from all foolish forms of bondage. Martin Luther stated: "The Christian is a most free lord of all, subject to none." But we must add that the Christian is under the law of love. In verse 14 Paul joins the two together. In Galatians 5:13 Paul makes the same point, and, to the similarly-troubled Corinthians, he wrote: "All things are lawful for me, but all things are not expedient."

The application of the law of love does not mean that we cease to be free. But it *does* mean that if we walk in love as well as in liberty we shall be preserved from using our liberty to indulge our selfishness. It all comes down to the issue of whether I am living on the basis of self-indulgence, or love. The Christian has the truly great privilege of surrendering his rights to the Lord.

We're strong on our "rights" in this generation, but we are weak on our duties. Many people quote the Martin Luther quotation I have just given you, but few go on to quote what he went on to say: "The Christian man is also a most dutiful servant of all, subject to all."

In verse 15 there's a compelling reason given us for the exercise of this brotherly love and consideration. Your brother is one for whom Christ died. Paul uses exactly the same argument and phrase in 1 Corinthians 8:11. How different, he emphasizes here, the careless hurtful attitudes we have to fellow believers, to the attitude Christ has to them! He loved them to the extent of dying to save them. There's an obvious contrast between the infinite sacrifice He made for this brother, and the trivial sacrifice I am unwilling to make for him.

As for the sixth element: *Let the things that matter to God be the things that matter to you*. That's the message of verse 17. Paul's real worry is highly relevent for the present time, a time in which so much time, mental energy, and resources have been expended on trivial, marginal issues. The evangelical church is brilliant at doing this. I once saw an advertisement for an American church which said: "We are a premillennial, dispensationalist, pre-tribulation, single rapture church and welcome all who are one with us in Christ." Do you see? We excel at allowing the marginal to become central.

To us, then, Paul asks: "Do you live and speak as if the marginal issues of Christian living and practices and ecclesiastical tradition were the central things?" Be assured, they are not! The great concerns of the church are the spiritual blessings of the gospel (verse 17), and *they* are the things that we're to get steamed up about. *Righteousness,* that inward quality of life in relationship to ourselves; *peace,* that quality of life in relation to others; *joy,* that quality of life in relation to God; these are the things that matter, and these priorities will shape our attitude to the church (verse 19) and to the work of God (verse 20).

The last strand of Paul's counsel is very simple: *If in doubt, don't!* (vv. 22–23). If you have a clear conscience, says Paul, then don't surrender your liberty. But don't brandish it— let it be between you and God. On the other hand, if the weak brother disregards his convictions for any other reason than the pressure of conviction, then he is sinning against God, because he doesn't really believe that what he is doing is right. If you have doubts about a course of action, don't do it, because you cannot act in faith. Act on principle, says Paul, never on expediency.

The great principle is the principle of faith. But faith, as it is depicted in Scripture, cannot be separated from obedience. It is faith in Jesus as Lord. The doctrine of the lordship of Christ is a key doctrine in this whole realm of Christian living. For our relationship with Him, with one another and with the world. It is the supreme banner under which we are to live; the banner of the absolute, universal, all-embracing lordship of Jesus.

CHAPTER 4
Romans 15:1-13

It is frequently said that Paul, at the beginning of Romans 15, is simply concluding the treatment of the question of doubtful things, which is the subject of chapter 14. But that subject is only touched on in 15:1, and it is touched on in order to lead into a much broader field of teaching. The general theme is a call for life focused on others rather than ourselves. This theme occupies the first thirteen verses of chapter 15, after which Paul turns to more personal, domestic matters.

Verse 1 is the link, with its emphasis on the duty of the strong in relation to the weak. Here Paul is not merely counseling patience with the infirmities of the weak and a good humored tolerance of their foibles; he is urging the strong to bear the infirmities of the weak in the sense of bearing and supporting those burdens. This is a great principle for every such relationship in any fellowship, however "strength" and "weakness" are to be interpreted.

You find that same principle at the beginning of Galatians 6, where the word "bear" does not mean simply "to tolerate," but rather to carry a load for someone. It's the rather lovely picture of those who are stronger within the fellowship showing such loving care for the weaker ones that they say, "Now, that's not a burden you should be carrying, let me get under it with you." That sort of attitude would solve so many of our problems. In Galatians 6:2, Paul shows that this burden-sharing is part of the law of Christ. It is an example of the selfless life focused on others for the glory of God, of which passage has much to say.

This is the alternative lifestyle and society which our Lord Jesus is building here, in our increasingly self-centered world. We are called to be members of that alternative society and to live that self-giving lifestyle for the sake of others, living not to please ourselves but to please our neighbor for his good.

This is not an inconsistent Pauline plea, that we should indulge in what he elsewhere condemns as "men-pleasing," as for example in Galatians 1:10 and Ephesians 6:6. The point, rather, is that there is more to be considered than the relative places of God and self in the soul. And I think that this is a very important thing to grasp. You see, a "pure motive," to please the Lord in the exercise of our Christian liberty, is not enough. It's a question of putting one's fellow-Christian above oneself. Sometimes this is the real test. In the words of the apostle John, "He who does not love his brother whom he has seen, how can he love God whom he has not seen?" (1 John 4:20).

In verse 2, Paul further defines the purity of this neighbor love of which he speaks by adding two qualifying phrases: "Let each of us please his neighbor *for his good, to edify him*." True neighbor love says, "I desire God's highest good for you." It needs guidelines, you notice. It is directed by a desire for God's glory in their lives for their good and to edify, to build them up, in Him. My whole heart is to be set on whatever will build my brother up in Christ. I am to shun whatever will draw him away from Christ, whatever will put a stumbling block in his way.

In verse 3, Paul cites the perfect example of this quality of selfless living: Jesus Christ. Another situation which comes to mind is in Philippians 2:5, where there is disagreement and self-seeking among some of the people in the Philippian church. Paul once again sets the example of Jesus before them, using the highest doctrine to commend the humblest duty. That, of course, is the great purpose of these glorious doctrines of the faith. In the economy of God, *doctrine* produces *character*. That is why it is important for us not to be lazy or superficial in our understanding of the great truths of the word of God. They are character-forming. The infinite selflessness of our Lord Jesus is therefore not only the means *of our justification*; it is the *pattern of our sanctification*.

And there has never been a more costly refusal to indulge self-interest. Paul finds a striking example of it in the psalm he quotes in verse 3. From Psalm 69, "The reproaches of those who reproached Thee have fallen on me." Remember Christ. His self-denial was of infinite proportion, says Paul, compared with the trivial irritation you are bearing. If Christ had pleased Himself and clung to the His privileges, where would *we* be?

There is a pattern here which is the key to fruitfulness both in life and in service to God. The pattern is the pattern of dying to self and living to God. Our Savior's death and resurrection are unique, in that they were redemptive. But, as Jesus illustrates in John 12:24, they are also a pattern for us.

So often, the central problem in our refusal to be like Jesus is a refusal to die to self. Yet the call of God is a call to die. Paul knew all the while, in the thousand deaths that he was called to die. Out of those deaths, the fruitfulness of his ministry sprang.

The quotation from Psalm 69 leads Paul to draw a more general lesson in verse 4. What he is speaking of in this verse is the relevance of Scripture. You get another example in 1 Corinthians 10, when, after a great account of the history of Israel, Paul says: "Now these things happened to them as a warning, but they were written down for our instruction." It is the instruction necessary for the fulfillment of our vocation in the will of God. So, when we are summoned, at the beginning of this section of Romans, into the will of God in all its fullness, that by the presentation of our bodies and the renewing of our minds and the transforming of our character, we might prove the will of God how are we to do this? Well, says the apostle, the instruction is from the word of God. You cannot just live this Christian way of life to which these chapters summon us, without constantly being under the ministry of the Scriptures. Seeking to live the Christian way of life divorced from this leads eventually to despair.

"That… we might have hope." You see, the demands of Scripture and the duties of the Christian life could so easily lead us into a spirit of hopelessness. How can we be delivered from that spirit? Well, he says in verse 4 that there are two things that we certainly need: "steadfastness" (that is, "perseverance") and "encouragement."

"Perseverance" is the same word you find at the beginning of Hebrews 12 — "let us run with *perseverance.*" We need perseverance. We need to "keep on." This word is one of the keywords of Christian living. In classical Greek, it's normally found either in a military context (like a man who does not flee the field of battle, but keeps on to the end), or in the context of athletics (like a runner in a race). This is the picture in Hebrews, and it is likewise the quality Paul longs for. Where do you find it? In God's word. God ministers perseverance to us through the Scriptures.

"Encouragement" is the same word as is used for the Holy Spirit in John 14, the "Paraclete," the one "called alongside." This is what Jesus saw the disciples were going to need. The Holy Spirit was going to come and be the encourager, to hold the burden up when it became too heavy, to take them on to the end. Significantly, these two words appear both in verses 4 and 5; the same words. In verse 4, they come from the Scripture; in verse 5, they come from God. The point is obvious. Perseverance and encouragement come from God. They are gifts to His children. But, and here is the point, the vessel in which God bears these blessings to His people is

Holy Scripture. This, He has decreed, is how He will minister perseverance and encouragement to us, so that we might live hopefully.

This is why we need to be continually absorbing God's word into our lives. So often, discouragement and hopelessness have their roots in a neglect of God's word. Through the Scriptures we come to know God in all His fullness. This is where we get in touch with His grace and sufficiency, His might and power, truth and glory. That's what the Bible is: It's the place where we come to know God. And that's the great need of our lives. With such a God as we have seen in His word, how shall we faint or fear?

But note also in verse 5 that God does not only keep His servants persevering and encouraged by the instruction of Scripture. He also uses the intercession of the saints. Verse 5 is not merely a wish. It is the expression of a prayer. Have you noticed how easily Paul in his epistles can move from exhortation to intercession? And here he is crying to the Lord for these Roman Christians, that they might live in harmony with each other, to the glory of the God and Father of our Lord Jesus Christ.

That's another way in which people may be kept going and be saved from discouragement. Praying was one of Paul's great ministries.

What does Paul pray for? He prays first for harmony in their fellowship. The phrase "in accord with Christ Jesus" is literally "to be minding the same things according to Christ Jesus" very reminiscent of the similar phrase in Philippians 2:5. Both there and in this chapter Paul is speaking of the harmony that derives from humility in accordance with Jesus' self-humbling. Paul prays that they might have a harmony that is in accordance with the mind of Jesus, and there is no true Christian harmony to be got any other way.

That harmony in the fellowship produces the other thing Paul prays for, which is unity in worship—"together... with one voice" (verse 6). I'm sure that here Paul is speaking about the common public worship, and there is much to learn from what he has to say.

We learn that true worship derives from the spiritual condition of God's people, by and large. That's why the secret of worship is not to be found in forms, whether old or new; it's to be found in being united by a common desire to glorify God through Jesus Christ. And the link with what has gone before is the example of the Lord Jesus, on the one hand *abasing Himself*, and on the other, *glorifying the Father*. So, after all these chapters about Christian character, Paul turns to speak about the kind of fellowship that together, with one voice, glorifies the God and Father of the Lord Jesus Christ.

Have you ever noticed what the people of God in heaven are doing at the throne of God, in the Book of Revelation? They are seeking to exalt God to the highest glory, and to humble themselves. You remember Elijah on Carmel, crying to God for rain? He is bowing down with his face to the ground and his head between his knees. You try that some time! The significance of it is that he can't get any lower than that. And that's how they're worshiping in heaven. Read Revelation 7. That's real worship. You don't get that from forms; it comes out of what God's grace has done in a man's character. He longs for the glory of God with all his being. It is the burning passion of his life. He longs to get as low as he can, to humble himself under God's mighty hand. And *that's* where God's people are worshiping. It happens in revival. God knows how we need this spirit of worship.

Now at the beginning of the second half of this passage, the apostle is widening the appeal not only to include the strong and the weak, but to include every kind of divisiveness which could arise in the church. Once again, Christ's example is normative. "Welcome one another, therefore as Christ has welcomed you, for the glory of God." It's not just an official welcome. It is a loving, costly giving of ourselves without stint to one another. That is what true Christian fellowship means. There are many practical implications of this. We need to ask, is this how fellowship really is experienced in our churches? I have seen lonely, introverted people, shy and perhaps unattractive, excluded by a phalanx of fellowship; by a group of Christians all sharing the good things they enjoy together, leaving the lonely Christians outside. True fellowship never springs from a life of self-pleasing, but from the heart of Jesus and His self-giving love.

If we are to follow Jesus' pattern, we are also to follow His motive: "...for the glory of God" (verse 7). Everything that Jesus did focused on that. Indeed throughout the Scriptures everything done by the Godhead conspires to that end. Have you ever thought of this? It was the design of the Father in creation. It was the design of the Son in the redemption of His people. And, says Paul, "We are being changed into the same image from glory into glory even as by the Spirit of God." God's great purpose is that everything might conspire to this end. There is nothing beyond this for the child of God. The glory of God is everything.

From verse 8, Paul elaborates on just how extensive Christ's welcome is. If the theme of verse 6 was worship, and the theme of verse 7 was fellowship, then the theme of verse 8 is the church's third great activity: *mission*. "Christ became a servant… in order that the Gentiles might glorify God for His mercy." Again, it is the nature of Christ's service who is a pattern for ours. We must go rather quickly through these verses, though I hope you will study them at your leisure. Paul is saying, from verse 8 onwards, that Christ came to the Jews for the Gentiles. This was the purpose and plan of God in sending a Savior. In other words, the salvation of the Gentiles was not an afterthought of God. It was this missionary vision and vocation that Christ had when He came into this world. Paul expounds this doctrine of mission in four stages.

First: *Christ became a servant* (verse 8). That's the basis of it. And it was not merely a title, it was an office He bore — compare again Philippians 2:7. That position is one we should adopt to each other. We are called to service and servanthood, because Christ became a servant. That's true of every one of us who are Christians.

Second: *He was sent to the Jews.* "I am not come," said Jesus to the Canaanite woman, "except to the lost house of Israel." Now there is a sense of this compulsion upon Jesus in His ministry, that He had been sent specifically to the Jews.

Third: *He was sent in the interests of God's covenant with Abraham.* It's an enormously important statement: "...in order to confirm the promises given to the patriarchs." There is a sense in which you cannot understand the meaning of Jesus' coming, apart from this. He came as a fulfillment of God's covenant promise to Abraham, which was sealed by circumcision — hence the reference in verse 8 to circumcision. There is a direct line, which Matthew points to in his genealogy, from Abraham to Bethlehem. At Bethlehem, God was mindful of His covenant. This is what they were singing about when Jesus was born. In Christ God is fulfilling His promise to Abraham. That's where the mercies of God reach back to.

And fourth: *He came ultimately in the interests of the salvation of the Gentiles* (verse 9). The Jew is reminded that (as Handley Moule puts it), "the promise of salvation, while given wholly through the Jew, was not given wholly for him." That was what Simeon was singing about in the temple: "A light, for revelation to the Gentiles." He gave the charter for missionary vocation there.

From verse 9, Paul reinforces this missionary vision with extensive quotations from Scripture (verses 9 to 12). It's not without significance that he quotes from the three sections of the Hebrew Bible

— the Law, the Prophets, and the Writings. Paul, you see, is urging on his people that the doctrine of mission is a Christian doctrine. The God of the Bible is not narrowly preoccupied either with our own little group or our own little nation. He is not the God of the Jews only, but the Gentiles also. And God's design was that the Gentiles should know His name, belong to His people, praise Him for His grace, and acknowledge His Lordship.

That's the biblical basis for mission, beloved. Paul is saying that the God of the Bible is a missionary God; the Christ of the gospel is a missionary Savior; that the Old Testament is a missionary book; and that the church is meant to be a missionary church. And that means a missionary obligation, laid on every church. Why? Well, Paul gives us here not just the biblical basis for the mission, but *the biblical motive for mission:* "…in order that the Gentiles might glorify God for His mercy."

Here again, the only ultimate motive is the glory of God. If I have shared in any real way in God's zeal and jealousy for His own glory, then my great desire will be to see God rightly glorified in every place, among every people. The fact that this is not yet the case is the greatest motive of mission. Does it matter to you that God is being robbed of His glory? Does it matter to you the way it mattered to Paul in Athens, when he saw the sophisticated Athenians giving themselves to idol worship? We read that Paul was "provoked in his spirit" — the same word that is used in medical Greek for a heart attack. Does it matter to you, all you that pass by?

That is the biblical motive for mission. In a way that is most fitting, then, the apostle provides us with our closing prayer in verse 13:

> "May the God of hope fill you with all joy and peace in believing, so that by the power of the Holy Spirit you may abound in hope."

How shall we live this Christian way of life? How shall we go into this sick world of ours and live like this, as the apostle has been describing to us? The answer is in that little phrase, "by the power of the Holy Spirit." Oh, may God grant us an access to that power, for the glorifying of His name in the world, and for the healing of the nations.

ALLIANCE
OF CONFESSING EVANGELICALS

The ALLIANCE OF CONFESSING EVANGELICALS is a coalition of believers who hold to the historic creeds and confessions of the Reformed faith and proclaim biblical doctrine in order to foster a Reformed awakening in today's Church.

AllianceNet.org